Life Through The Eyes Of An Insider

101 Poems to help you understand life better

By Terry Lander

Published by Lyvit Publishing, Cornwall

www.lyvit.com

ISBN 978-0-9555061-1-6

None of the poems included in this book are related to actual places, persons or events except the content of 'Kernow' and 'Shameless Plug', and any resemblance to anything or anyone, living or dead is entirely coincidental.

No Part of this book may be reproduced in any way, including, but not limited to, electronic or mechanical copying, photocopying, recording or by any information storage or retrieval system now known or hereafter invented, without prior consent from the publisher.

This book is sold subject to the condition that it shall not, by way of trade or otherwise, be lent, re-sold, hired out or otherwise circulated without the publisher's prior consent in any form of binding or cover other than that in which it is published and without a similar condition including this condition being imposed on the subsequent purchaser.

All Material Including Cover Design © Terry Lander 2005

"I'm not aspiring to be someone else – If I'm me for the rest of my life then so be it"

To Caewyn, who took so little but gave so much.

Also to my wife, Mary, and my son, Joe, for putting up with me during the production, an unenviable task.

Contents

1. Animal Lives
2. Mugging
3. Christmas Time
4. Beach Trip
5. Top Job
6. It's For You
7. Goldfish
8. Down
9. Post Time
10. Things People Wear
11. Hamster
12. Surprise!
13. The Dragon
14. Loopy Kids
15. Newborn
16. Anti-Bacterial Action
17. Unwanted
18. Kernow
19. Similar Interests
20. Granddad
21. Big Spender
22. Our Tree
23. Pet Perils
24. My Old PAL
25. Bar-Room Brawl
26. Chocoholic
27. Plane Crash
28. Train Ride
29. Dad and Sport
30. Real Love
31. Tenner Dilemma
32. College Football
33. Match Day
34. Robbery

Contents

35. You
36. Footsie
37. Shopping List
38. Nearly On Track
39. Beard Bothers
40. The Simple Life
41. Sled Race
42. Hard Time
43. Coloured World
44. Easy Life
45. We Have a Loser
46. The Park
47. Astrology
48. Help With the Housework
49. Lucky Neighbour
50. Hit the Sales
51. Cute Canine
52. Stress
53. Debt Busters
54. Wall Rivalry
55. Instructions
56. Forbidden Passion
57. Time of the Month
58. Sweet Course
59. Cedric
60. Voices
61. Religious Concerns
62. Time Out
63. Clothing Issues
64. Same Ol' Same Ol'
65. Directions
66. Credit Rating
67. Mime
68. Ironing

Contents

69. Motor Ways
70. Flowers
71. Problem?
72. Crockery Shock
73. Dope on A Soap
74. Space Rockers
75. Employment
76. Family Recipe
77. My Mrs
78. Floor Flaws
79. Fencing
80. Computer
81. PC Pleasure
82. Shave Time
83. 'Net Fever
84. The Inventor
85. Limited Edition
86. Hibernation
87. Literature Tale
88. Toys
89. Car Trouble
90. Ted
91. Empty Shelves
92. Waking Nightmare
93. Broom Cupboard Fantasies
94. Town Planning
95. Photographer
96. New Home
97. Decisions
98. Taboo
99. Check-up
100. British Institution
101. Shameless Plug

Animal Lives

What do animals do all day
When they're not eating or sleeping?
They don't need to rush to their work
Or worry about time keeping

Since they don't have a long routine
What else must they do with their day?
If they want to mate they do it
Without practising what to say

There's nothing but hours for them
As they don't have a list of chores
Nothing to cook, no dishes and
No things to put back in their drawers

They don't have much to do of a night
Their whole evening looks to be free
They don't bring their work home with them
As happens so often with me

While envying them for all this
I think about my spare evenings
When I go out to meet my friends
And talk 'til everyone's leaving

Although it would be inviting
To have all the time going spare
The sacrifices that I'd make
Would be too difficult to bear

TV would go, along with books
Cinema and theatre too
Relationships we've worked to build
Would never exist as they do

So I've taken a look at life
And how animals spend the day
I've learnt that we have it so good
And I'm sure I'd keep it this way

Mugging

While walking down the street one day
I saw a weird sight
A reverend jumped an old woman
Though she put up a fight

He struggled for a little while
As I was running there
He pulled the old girl to the floor
And dragged her by her hair

I shouted out which scared him off
Although he had her bag
He ran quite fast and dodged the crowd
Then threw away his fag

Policemen turned up at the scene
And took the facts from us
"It all happened so fast", we said
A line that makes them cuss

So no I.D. was ever made
To catch the crook that day
The woman's bag was gone for good
The reverend got away

Christmas Time

Why do some people eat so much
Through Christmas and New Year
They'll fill themselves with buffet food
And wash it down with beer

There's biscuits and selection packs
That they'll throw down their throat
And then they find they've put on weight
So buy a bigger coat

I don't mind all the festive cheer
I'm always in the mood
It would just be a help to know
Why it's not next year's food

Beach Trip

I sat on the beach one morning
Looking towards the sea
I saw a swimmer struggling
Shouting, "Someone, Help me"

I watched him kick and flap his arms
As he began to drown
No one else had noticed him
He started going down

He reminded me of myself
All helpless and alone
Like when I had my accident
And should have been at home

I was hit by a drunk driver
It's nothing I did wrong
I lay there helpless afterwards
Was in pain for so long

I watched the swimmer lose his fight
And then I realised
It was that awful accident
That left me paralysed.

Top Job

The best position I could fill
Is as a Film Critic
As they tell people what they think
And if films make them sick

I'd like to be at the pictures
With such great company
And sit there knowing you're at work
With popcorn that is free

It's For You

Why does everyone have to ring
When I've gone up to bed
They have a day before to phone
I need to rest my head

I wouldn't bother answering
But someone could be hurt
No, it's just my old mum again
She's digging for some dirt

Goldfish

My name's Frederick, Fred to you
I'm a goldfish you see
I've got about three seconds left
To tell you what happens to me

My name's Frederick, Fred to you
I'm a goldfish you see
I've got about three seconds left
To tell you what happens to me

My name's Frederick…

Down

Down as an Eskimo chewing on ice
Down as a father of thirteen with lice
Down as a lion that's found it's no good
Down as a tree that ends up as driftwood

Down as a driver who's lost his licence
Down as a fat man who has no Y-fronts
Down as a car on its last dregs of fuel
Down as a rapper who's told he's not cool

Down as an explorer missing his home
Down as a garden with no fishing gnome
Down as a tele with just five channels
Down as a van with only two panels

Down as a policeman with no speeders
Down as a bluebird looking for feeders
Down as a camper who's kit disappears
Down as a baby who's born with no ears

Down as a climber who's run out of rock
Down as a captain who's just hit the dock
Down as a victim that's just lost his wife
Down as another who will lose their life

Post time

I like to hear the postman come
To see what gifts he brings
I often send for free samples
Of hair shampoo and things

His visit always cheers me up
It's my cure when I'm ill
I wonder what he's brought today
Oh – I forgot the bills

Things people wear

The girl who lives in number twelve
Wears tons of jewellery
I'm shocked that she can stand up straight
Opposing gravity

She has four sets of hoop earrings
And two studs in her nose
It's always sandals that she wears
With rings around her toes

She's got a ring for each finger
And most of them have stones
With all the necklaces she wears
She looks like traffic cones

I think she's got a belly bar
I'm sure that you'd agree
What she wears is over the top
But rather her than me

Hamster

In and out
Up the barrel
Through the hoop
Over Carole

Back around
Under the stairs
Dodge and weave
Avoid the chairs

To the box
Everything's fine
Hammy has
Made record time

Surprise!

I detest buying birthday gifts
It's more than I can take
Normally when their time comes round
I give a gift I make

This year I hope to try harder
And give gifts from the heart
My Dad's birthday is coming up
I want to get him darts

I'll go shopping in the morning
As I'm at work from one
I could get everybody's gifts
So that the year is done

Well, that was a nice idea
But I forgot to go
I'll have to make him something good
Or take him to a show

The Dragon

Donny was a strange dragon
Who was scared of mice
He always stank of whisky
And was cursed with lice

He hated chasing people
As they laughed at him
And all the stupid beach kids
Kicked him in his shins

He was a lazy lizard
But he didn't care
He just smoked and drank all day
In his underwear

Then, one day, something changed
He looked at the sand
To see a female dragon
Slowly getting tanned

Donny had hit the jackpot
As he asked her out
He made her life like a queen's
Loved her without doubt

Now Donny stays clean-shaven
Though life isn't fun
His missus has him well trained
He's under her thumb

Loopy Kids

Kids try to drive you up the wall
And also round the bend
They'll make you do a loop-the-loop
That never seems to end

They'll make you totally crazy
Nuts and bonkers too
They'll send you more or less ga-ga
Until you've gone cuckoo

They'll carry on 'til you're barmy
And both your eyes spin round
They'll make sure that you're round the twist
And you can't touch the ground

Then just before you go mental
And want to flip your lid
They show you just how cute they are
Besides, they are your kids

Newborn

Everyone thought baby was cute
All tucked up in his bed
What they missed from beside the cot
Were the thoughts inside his head

He dreamt of ruling the whole world
Everybody's leader
He understood the stock market
And was a perfect reader

He had a laser in his room
Hidden by his teddy
All it needed was charging up
Before it would be ready

His army was contactable
Via his radio
Hidden within his monitor
So his parents didn't know

There he lies with his deadly tools
Waiting for the hour
To tell his allies it is time
To lead him into power

Anti-Bacterial Action

We seem to make our kids lives worse
By being far too clean
We wash, rewash, then rinse as well
Then use some cleaning cream

By killing ninety nine per cent
Of bugs that hang about
Our children won't take any germs
And then can't sort them out

This means their poor antibodies
Quickly become too old
They'll pick up every infection
And then can't shift their colds

Unwanted

The butterfly flew in to town
To get his kids some bread
But when he got into the store
The shopkeeper was dead

He looked around the other shops
And each time found the same
Everybody had been shot dead
As if they were all game

He got distraught when he saw that
Policemen were dead too
Everything was silent that day
Even the local zoo

The butterfly then flew back home
A tear rolled down his face
He left the town in such a mess
A really sad disgrace

When he had gone the townspeople
Went home to get cleaned up
They hate that butterfly so much
They hid under ketchup

Kernow

Cornwall's beauty can be summed up
By using just one word
Spectacular, incredible
Amazing and absurd

It's marvellous, unbeatable
The best in all the land
Fantastic, gorgeous, wonderful
Almighty, great and grand

It's traditional, perfection
A sight that must be seen
Influential, natural, lush
Charming, stunning and green

It's fresh, majestic, bounteous
Pure, unspoilt for miles
Quaint, historic, uncontested
So why not stay a while

Similar Interests

I've got myself a brand new girl
And we hate to be apart
I take her out to classy joints
Like rugby practice and darts

She loves it when we go fishing
Much more when she gets a bite
I want to take her to a club
I'll see if she's free tonight

I wonder what she'll wear for me
Maybe a short skirt and boots
They've got a secret agent theme
So the men will be in suits

I phoned her up and she chucked me
I didn't know what to say
She's just lucky she got there first
I'd have chucked her anyway

Granddad

My granddad fought in World War two
Well, fought is not quite right
He heard the loud bang of a gun
And it gave him a fright

Instantly he went to the floor
They all thought he was dead
Everything was, effectively
Except that in his head

He lay down there in total shock
His eyes were tightly closed
He was there for about a week
No threat to him was posed

After that time my granddad woke
And put his backpack on
He tried to make it back to camp
But saw that it had gone

He was posted to war quite late
Due to a minor flaw
The carrier that had his note
Was killed outside his door

The last few days of awfulness
Were all that he had known
The war was won within that week
He had just to get home

Big Spender

I always spend my hard earned cash
On really useless junk
I've just bought two stuffed animals
A badger and chipmunk

I bought an antique calendar
From eighteen eighty two
I've also got an old scrapbook
Of naval guy's tattoos

I've got a worn out steering wheel
That's made from antique wood
I really should have left it there
It isn't any good

The biggest problem with it all
Is all the room it takes
I'll advertise the lot of it
And see how much it makes

Our Tree

For the tree
Who stands around
Making air
While holding ground

Keeping birds
Away from cats
Holding on
To sleeping bats

Humble tree
Who's always good
Come with me
For firewood

Pet Perils

Pets can be quite funny
When they're running around
I've always noticed ours
Try digging through the ground

I wonder what I do
That makes them run away
I give them fresh water
And feed them every day

I take them to the vet
And always keep them clean
I wonder what it is
That makes them think I'm mean

I make sure they can move
By giving them their space
Maybe they are put off
By my hideous face

My Old PAL

Videos are being replaced
With smaller DVD's
They say the pictures much better
With higher quality

But when I want to go to bed
And haven't seen the end
I always find it difficult
To find my place again

Bar-Room Brawl

Tempers are flared
Rage is high
A punch is thrown
Which knocks out a guy

His mate stands up
Throws his fist
Goes for the scum
But finds he's missed

He hits the floor
Goes to sleep
He's made the count
And won't make a peep

Tables are thrown
Hit three more
A chair's thrown back
The guy meets the floor

A man is thrown
Finds the bar
All of a sudden
The wall meets a car

It's through the wall
Run over four
Now there's beer, blood
And glass on the floor

The barmaid's heard
And come back
She's closed her fist
And giving out smacks

Faster they fall
There's no end
She's just clocked out
And lies on my friend

During all this
I just prayed
I'm happy now
As I never paid

Chocoholic

Chocolate is my favourite pastime
It always makes me weak
If I'm having any problem
It's chocolate that I seek

I usually have one bar spare
That I keep next to me
It's like a final cigarette
Every day I have three

I know this may seem quite normal
As these things often can
The only complication is
The fact that I'm a man

Plane crash

I was in an aeroplane
When it suddenly had to dive
It got caught up in a storm
It's a shame I didn't survive

Train Ride

The train pulled out of the station
On it's route by the coast
It was sunny and beautiful
A day it loved the most

Over the hills and through tunnels
Into valleys as well
Greeting everyone that it met
With a ring of it's bell

Passing through so many stations
Picking people up too
Past the beaches full of tourists
Some in the sea, so blue

They finally reached their last stop
And rested at the gate
The passengers were running now
The train had got there late

Dad and Sport

My Dad watches all kinds of sport
From football to rugby
He'll watch the cricket and the golf
That's shown on the TV

He'll watch the pay-per-view boxing
As long as it is cheap
And best of all he'll watch the lot
While catching up on sleep

Real Love

I love to feel your tender kiss
Wherever we may be
Even when the football's on
And my team's on TV

I like to feel it when we're out
And it's just us alone
I never mind admitting that
It sometimes makes me moan

Your sweet taste as we gently touch
Brings out the best in me
My favourite place for us to meet
Is right next to the sea

The sand between my toes is great
But perfect with you, dear
I've given up my friends for you
My true love that is beer

Tenner Dilemma

I've just found ten pounds on the floor
I wish I'd left it there
The problem hanging over me
Is whether I should care

I think that I should hand it in
As if it were some keys
But maybe I should pocket it
Although they might see me

I'd hand it to the local shop
But there's a massive line
Hang on – I think I've lost ten pounds
Then this one must be mine

College Football

When playing football with my mates
They always laugh at me
When I go for the top corner
The ball lands in a tree

I try to hit the inside post
So it will rocket in
But normally it rockets out
And smacks somebody's chin

So now I'm reduced to crossing
And everyone else scores
I just need to control the ball
And then I'll score some more

I've just been passed the ball to cross
I'll dribble it instead
I've gone for the shot, inside post
And hit somebody's head

Match Day

It rained on the day of the match
But that didn't get to us
We were set to watch our boys win
As we clambered on the bus

Jimmy knew where he was going
So he was told he could drive
We left that day at half past ten
As the match kicked off at five

We arrived with no time to spare
As Jimmy hadn't a clue
Kick off was in twenty minutes
We ran as though storms were due

All seemed still for such a big game
But we didn't seem to see
We had to get into our seats
To fulfil our destiny

As we got closer to the ground
Our spirits finally dogged
'The match is off' the closed gates said
The whole pitch was waterlogged

Robbery

I've come into my local bank
So I can rob the place
I've planned to do it subtlely
And at a steady pace

I'll hand a note to the teller
Demanding all the cash
It tells her not to make a scene
As then I'll make a dash

Just one more person in the queue
And then it's party time
Oh no! Robbers have stormed the bank
To do their evil crime

I hope they don't shoot anyone
Or more precisely me
I'll just stay on the ground right here
And do it quietly

The first robber has left the bank
The second's running out
If I can pull him to the ground
Then I'll give him a clout

I've done it! He is now out cold
Lying down on the floor
The first one must have got away
The cops are through the door

The bank staff called me a hero
And offered me a boat
The cops are searching witnesses
Oh no! That stupid note!

You

You're my up when I feel down
You make me smile instead of frown
You're my right when I am wrong
You shorten me when I'm too long

You're my here when I am there
And my clothing when I feel bare
You're my big when I am small
And my yes when I'm not at all

You're my good when I feel bad
And my calm when I'm feeling mad
You're my can when we just can't
And my are when we really aren't

You're the bright that aids my gloom
And the hope that sees off the doom
You're the land when I'm at sea
You're the perfect person for me

Footsie

I never understood Wall Street
Or what they do up there
I just know it's something to do
With dealing stocks and shares

I asked around and no one knew
So I read the FT
I threw that jargon in the bin
And know it's not for me

Shopping List

When I went shopping
I forgot some things
Bread, sugar, milk, marg,
Spicy chicken wings

Chocolate, biscuits, crisps
Poisson á la crème
Lemonade and juice
I'd best go back again

Nearly on Track

If I could have just seven grand
Then I'd pay off my loan
I need two hundred grand on top
So I can buy my home

Another ten would see me right
To buy a decent car
I'd need a steady income then
So some to buy a bar

Once I've purchased the stuff I need
I can start to relax
I think I've overlooked one thing
Can you pay off my tax?

Beard Bothers

I'm glad I haven't got a beard
A silly, hairy face
I'd hate to have to keep it groomed
With every hair in place

I'd hate it when my beard when grey
I'd just have to dye it
However, as my name's Danielle
I can't even try it

The Simple Life

Bin, when I stop to think about
The way you live your life
You eat the good bits I can't have
As you don't have a wife

I'd quite enjoy the fat from meat
And jelly from the ham
I envy you so much, my friend
I'd love the mouldy jam

Sled race

Sledding is a popular sport
For us in the South West
We hold a one-day sledding race
To find out who's the best

We train throughout the whole morning
And give the winner beer
We'd try to make it longer, but
It snows one day a year

Hard Time

I was always bullied at school
For being overweight
They used to flush me down the loo
And hang me on the gate

I tried to cut down on my food
But wasn't helped by Dad
He still put chocolate in my lunch
Said, "You're a growing lad"

So every day it was the same
Pokes and taunts until one
After lunch it always got worse
They never were quite done

One day I stood up for myself
By then I'd had enough
I turned round to the ringleader
And grabbed him by the scruff

I told him not to bully me
Or I would break his spine
Then our head teacher changed his job
I'd got him to resign

Coloured world

Pink elephants
And orange bats
Mauve kangaroos
And yellow cats

Turquoise badgers
And day-glo bugs
Crimson horses
And navy slugs

Dark green giraffes
With light green chins
Oh, if I'd coloured
The animals in

Easy Life

The lighthouse has a perfect job
It just shows a warning
The lucky thing's a part-timer
Which sleeps past the morning

I guess it must be nocturnal
It doesn't see the day
I guess I wouldn't want it's job
I hear it's awful pay

We Have a Loser

I was driving my car around
Just spending time on my own
Then I saw a 'King of the Road'
Who should have stayed on his throne

He beeped at me and flashed his lights
As I wasn't fast enough
But I was at the speed limit
Which got him into a huff

He kept trying to overtake
And nearly hit someone's car
I don't know why some people can't
Just stay behind where they are

He offered me the 'V' signal
And was mouthing through the glass
As if I'd speed up any more
Or let the idiot pass

Finally it was safe for him
He pulled his car around mine
Then the blue lights started to flash
That's three points and a big fine

The Park

Everybody enjoys the park
As there's so much to do
It's not just fun for the children
Adults can join in too

Basic parks have a slide and swings
But some have even more
Like roundabouts you push yourself
And sometimes a trap door

Climbing frames are often present
And they've got different things
Like tunnels, rope ladders and poles
And sometimes hanging rings

With all the stuff you'll find at parks
It's worth a try, trust me
You'll also find that at the park
All the features are free

Astrology

I like to read my horoscope
To see how life will change
Then I know what to keep the same
And what to rearrange

Today I'll face some challenges
And meet a brand new friend
We'll have so much in common that
We'll want to meet again

Apparently I'll change my job
And I'll be my own boss
The company will miss me though
Never mind, it's their loss

Well, that day's over and I found
My horoscope was wrong
Today was just like yesterday
I knew it all along

Help With the Housework

I wish I had a thousand arms
So I could do my chores
It would save me running around
And giving my feet sores

I could clean the whole of the house
Before the clock hit ten
That would leave the rest of the day
To chill out with my friends

But the problems I'd encounter
Would be more than a few
I doubt I could control them all
I think I'll stick with two

Lucky Neighbour

My neighbour's won the lottery
And built on to his home
His castle's lying dormant now
As they've both gone to Rome

The speedboat on his new trailer
Suggests he's won a lot
Apparently last Saturday
Was such a large jackpot

I wouldn't say that I'm jealous
Though secretly I am
As his rusty pile of rubbish
Is now a new Trans-Am

The jewellery hanging off his wife
Must have cost her a mint
I'd buy my wife a diamond ring
But it would leave me skint

His snotty little satans
Are sporting brand new gear
I'm shocked his acre of garden
Isn't full with reindeer

I think they're back from Rome today
And someone's at his door
It's a man in a suit and tie
Perhaps he's won some more

I'm looking at the guy closely
And the police nearby
Billy's been done for burglary
His lake of luck's run dry

Hit the Sales

Bargains are a brilliant way
Of filling up your shelves
You don't know that you're doing it
'Til you've got eighteen elves

You'll buy so many DVDs
You won't know what to watch
And loads of flat-pack furniture
To help your husband botch

You'll end up with so much about
There'll be nowhere to sleep
But you won't mind how much it cost
Because it was so cheap

Cute Canine

I wish I were the loo roll dog
Just to get the cuddles
I would like to spend all day
Splashing in the puddles

I'd love to live with all his fame
And no threat of failure
I bet with every shoot he does
He gets his own trailer

Stress

I think I'm getting an ulcer
From all the daily stress
I try to sort out both our kids
But I just get depressed

I can't wait until they're eighteen
As they can then move out
Until then it's just Me V. Them
And they'll win without doubt

Debt Busters

This is for the loan companies
Who seem to follow me
I've seen your adverts hanging round
On billboards and TV

Now I've got your contact number
Please just leave me alone
And when I find myself in debt
I'LL give YOU a phone

Wall Rivalry

The wall was jealous of the house
As it's warm all the time
But as the wall was stuck outside
It always got the grime

People wanted to walk on it
Which meant it's stones fell out
And then there were the bad drivers
Who gave the wall a clout

One day it decided to leave
And hide out in the school
The only problem that it found
Was that it is a wall

Instructions

If I die before I wake
Make sure I'm gone for goodness sake
Ask a doctor to confirm
I've carried out my final term
If you can then bury me
Just make sure that I'm near a tree
Get the buffet under way
Half way through this fantastic day
Everyone will follow you
So smile, as I know you'll get through
Make sure that the hot DJ
Knows exactly which songs to play
To keep spirits off the ground
And make sure you enjoy your round
Now I've got this down, my wife
I'm off to get the best of life

Forbidden Passion

I loved you from when we first met
As I saw deep in your eyes
I looked your body up and down
A look I couldn't disguise

My dear, you were so ravishing
Voluptuous if I may
I hoped you went for men like me
And wouldn't push me away

You were so shy and sensitive
Qualities that I adore
You didn't say that much to me
Which left me begging for more

You had to beat men off with sticks
Or anything that you found
You wowed me when you knocked one out
And he fell straight to the ground

But now you've told me we can't be
Due to a bump in the road
You're a gorgeous beauty queen
And I'm a rare Scottish toad

Time of the Month

I've got bills coming out of my ears
Sometimes too many to cope
The water, gas and electric
Know just how to drain my hope

Then there are the clubs who offer
Twelve books for the price of six
Then you pay through the nose for more
I'm sick of their sneaky tricks

Credit cards have so many 'deals'
Like naught per cent for a time
The trouble is they're not paid off
And some then resort to crime

Loans to pay off all your debts
Are what really make me itch
To get yourself a worthwhile rate
You have to prove that you're rich

So I'll keep on until I'm clear
But I doubt that will be soon
Just a note to the banks out there
Go find some other baboon

Sweet Course

My favourite ice cream flavour's mint
I also like vanilla
I'd like to eat every dessert
That's come out of the chiller

Rum and raisin's a specialty
Although I'll eat that as well
I love the taste of strawberry
In delicious wafer shells

A whippy in a double cone
Topped off with a sauce and flake
Is perfect when you're on the beach
As long as it doesn't break

It's not just ice cream that I like
Cheesecakes are great to have too
As long as they're put in a bowl
With ice cream, stirred 'til its goo

And Pavlovas are luxury
With all that gorgeous meringue
And mint ice cream perched on the side
Oops – I'm back where I began

Cedric

Cedric the van was feeling down
He wasn't even awake
Then his driver opened the shed
They had lots of stops to make

So Cedric trundled off on route
To make the first of his stops
Suddenly his cab filled with smoke
As he felt his engine pop

His driver found that he was dry
There was no water in him
His radiator was no good
He went the same way as Tim

Now Cedric has been recycled
But hasn't become a train
It's just a shame he's scared of heights
He's the bottom of a plane

Voices

I've got these voices in my head
They're telling me to do things
Like cooking, cleaning, washing up
And buying expensive rings

The doctor's told me she can't help
My psychiatrist has too
They'd love to help me with my woes
But wouldn't know what to do

The medium just said the same
So it can't be ghosts or ghouls
It's not the guy who's in my dreams
The one who chuckles and drools

They're not the voices of loves lost
As I've never lost a love
There is no voice of our old dog
Who's now living high above

I think I've found the owners of
The voices that rule my life
Most belong to my whinging kids
The other's my nagging wife

Religious Concerns

I've often thought about dying
And whether there's a heaven
Are we blessed with nine lives, like cats
Or maybe only seven

Will I be reincarnated
As someone who's in power
Or will I end up as a gnat
And live for just an hour

Maybe our life just finishes
And when we're gone it's the end
Or maybe we go back in time
And I'll become Churchill's friend

Either way it's worrying me
About what happens to us
I guess I'll find out soon enough
I've just been hit by a bus

Time out

I love to watch the world go by
As I just sit there staring
Children on their skateboards do tricks
And each one gets more daring

Then there's the ladies as they fight
On the market stalls outside
"That's my dress", "No it's not, it's mine"
"Ambulance there, wanna ride?"

My favourites are the so-called 'gangs'
Who seem too fearful to fight
They hang around when everyone's gone
Usually last thing at night

When the pubs close there's some action
As one bloke nicks his mates girl
"I'll cave your head in, idiot,
Nobody touches my Shirl"

No one seems to notice me much
As I watch them walk about
And that suits me just fine, really
As I'll never make it out

Clothing Issues

How did we end up wearing clothes
When animals don't care?
They wake up and get on with it
While we choose what to wear

Why do we spend that time in shops
Trying to look our best
I've never seen an elephant
Complain about his vest

I find that when it comes to clothes
Some have poor attitudes
But then, I'd rather deal with that
Than walk round in the nude

Same Ol' Same Ol'

I've been stuck in this job for months
And every day's the same
I'm sure that I'm well qualified
It really is a shame

All I do is photocopy
Documents for others
I should have got a decent job
Working for my brothers

But pride got in the way of that
And now I'm here instead
I really want to work from home
So I can stay in bed

I could have gone to the army
Although I'm scared of tanks
Oh, what's the point in self-pity
I'm off to rob the bank

Directions

I asked a guy how we could get
To my friend's house one day
I have to say I was amazed
With what he had to say

"I think it's left on this 'ere road
But then it could be that 'un
You'll need to go right past the barn
With a swinging baton"

"Make sure you follow this 'ere path
To get a decent ride"
I must say he was nice enough
But we were parked outside

Credit Rating

I have so many credit cards
That I have built a house
I live there with my faithful pet
Dominic the dormouse

Although I have to pay them off
Along with my new fridge
They've all got low, fixed interest rates
So I have no mortgage

Mime

Anyone
Who's out there
Look at me
Stop and stare

This is my
Only time
To get cash
I'm a mime

If you don't
I'll give chase
Just to watch
Your red face

If you do
Fifty pee
Will get you
Smiles from me

Ironing

Ironing's a horrendous chore
I hate with a passion
I can find no better way of
Ruining your fashion

It always seems to take an age
To find the final shirt
Sometimes I'd rather leave them creased
And caked with thick, black dirt

Motor Ways

My friend's just bought a GTI
It's a new three litre
It does two hundred miles an hour
No one else can beat her

Her mate's got a pulsing V6
And it's been bored out too
Naught to sixty in five seconds
It turns the tarmac blue

My best friend's car has two engines
Between the front and rear
When it's barrelling at top speed
I'm sure that it won't steer

Mine's got much less under the front
You may say that it's slow
But I take mine out every day
It keeps me on the road

Besides the top speed limit here
Goes up to seventy
Their performance is wasted as
They can't overtake me

Flowers

Flowers must live an awful life
As men give them away
And bees act like their new best mate
To steal pollen in May

There's not a flower doctor yet
To rid them of green fly
So they are eaten, leaves and all
And left until they die

I hope this does not put you off
But please give them good care
Because if you just leave the flies
They'll no longer be there

Problem?

Problem pages are laughable
As each one is a clone
They're full of people with loved ones
Who leave the family home

Then there's the guys who can't get dates
I think, "Well go out, fool"
And finally the lonely kids
Who hate to go to school

I like to sit and mock them all
As their lives are so sad
What's this? A letter from my wife
She's living with my Dad!

I'll see if I can get her back
By writing to 'Dear Sue'
I'll send a letter off to her
She'll tell me what to do

Crockery Shock

Life is better with paper plates
As there's no washing up
We could also use paper bowls
As well as paper cups

When used they can be recycled
Then used again some more
It also saves the cleaning up
When they're dropped on the floor

Dope on a Soap

Soaps seem so unrealistic
From the character's point of view
So much happens to them each day
They wouldn't survive what they do

Take Flo from the soap 'The Midlands'
Whose parents were killed just last year
Her uncle's just become her aunt
Who pushed her best friend off the pier

She then passed her driving exam
And took her instructor to bed
That was behind her boyfriend's back
While surgeon's cut open his head

Once they removed his big tumour
And he was allowed back to work
His boss took on an apprentice
A lanky, hairy lad named Dirk

Now Dirk and he are an item
While Flo emigrated to Spain
But next week Dirk will be murdered
By the psycho who drives the train

These problems alone would be grim
But together would be much worse
Still, I'll be watching as always
I'm under the soap's wretched curse

Space Rockers

I've been driving around in space
With my band 'The Foursome'
I knew these space wagons were good
But this one is awesome

Everything looks the same out here
Now I think earth has gone
I'd better check the map I bought
To get to the M1

Ah, here's the problem, I went right
And headed straight for Crewe
We'd better get back to the bar
We've got a gig to do

Employment

A job is like the lottery
When you have just begun
Although one thing is guaranteed
You'll make tea on day one

They get you on to harder things
Though you can't match their pace
They're always seeming to forget
That you're not in a race

They try and offload boring jobs
That they don't want to do
Then you're pulled up as you forgot
The task assigned to you

If you find your workload's perfect
And you don't have to dash
The boss will make it twice as hard
Without the extra cash

When you're a master at your job
And they stop complaining
A new guy joins the company
And you'll do the training

Family Recipe

I'd like to try new recipes
When I'm making the tea
The problem is which one to do
To please the family

Spaghetti Bolognaise is out
As Dan hates tomatoes
And when our baby, Matt, eats it
He gets it up his nose

Any kind of curry's no good
Mike's allergic to rice
I'd give him boiled spuds instead
Although he hates the spice

I'd make an Olive Stroganoff
But they'd moan at the pips
I guess they'll have to stick with good
Ol' sausage, egg and chips

My Mrs

My wife is always going on
About the work she does
She looks after our home and son
And rarely gets a buzz

So I quit work, she got a job
And off she went that day
I helped our son play with his toys
Things were going my way

I left my chores 'til late that night
I had so much to do
All hell broke loose before too long
The boy escaped my view

He broke the plates and made a mess
With all the cleaning stuff
He got himself beneath our bed
And came out caked in fluff

My wife came back at half past six
The house was far from right
I had to make the place ship-shape
So cleaned throughout the night

Now she's happy in her new job
For her, at least, life's well
But I am stuck at home all day
Living a life of hell

Floor Flaws

The ceiling's always laughing at
The stupid downstairs floor
He sits up there, safe from all harm
And never feels the wars

The owners keep scraping their feet
Which makes the poor floor ache
He wishes they'd be more careful
Take pride for goodness sake

None of them know just how badly
Their old floor is feeling
But they've come through the upstairs floor
There goes their smug ceiling

Fencing

The fence lives such a long, cruel life
I don't know how it copes
It must just sit there all day long
Pretending not to mope

It gets a beating every time
We throw the big gate closed
And when it gets a winter cold
It suffers with it's nose

I'd give it a coat of varnish
To keep the poor thing warm
However, there's some cloud cover
Looks like we'll have a storm

Computer

The computer's taken over my life
I don't even watch TV
I haven't got time to write this poem
I can hear it calling me

PC Pleasure

My computer's so important
To help me work each day
It does all my arithmetic
And keeps mistakes at bay

My job would take about a week
Without my desktop friend
I'd have to do the work myself
My day would never end

I've just found a problem with it
And so I have to dash
It takes me three hours to sort
When they decide to crash

Shave Time

I have to say to all young lads
That shaving isn't great
A good friend that I knew from school
Was shaving from age eight

He started to grow up too fast
During a holiday
And by the time a month had gone
He did it every day

But by the time that lad was ten
He knew what we all feared
He got bored with shaving each day
And grew up with a beard

'Net fever

The Internet's a useful tool
With sites for everyone
I always find when I come off
I'm usually not done

I've forgotten how we managed
Before we had email
And auction sites are handy too
My brother's up for sale

The Inventor

When I was young I was quite good
At thinking up new things
The products that I thought about
Seemed so interesting

As I was no good at drawing
I just let them all die
But someone must think they're all good
As they're around to buy

Limited Edition

Collectables are loads of fun
It's great to get a set
I often wonder what they're worth
Though I won't sell them yet

I've got an antiques valuer
Coming this afternoon
So I've collected all my sets
And put them in one room

Well he's just been and I must say
That was a waste of time
He called them all future antiques
So they're not worth a dime

Hibernation

The mice were out collecting food
So they could hibernate
They were looking around the rooms
For tasty nuts and dates

Whilst gathering them in their hole
They found a massive flaw
The cat had mastered power tools
And cut himself a door

By the time the poor mice noticed
The cat was nearly through
Good job one had a flamethrower
He'd set to gas mark two

Literature Tale

I could read a million books
As each one is a gem
I'd love to sit there in a room
And make my way through them

My favourite book of all time is
'Action' by Rick Murrsion
But when I say I read the books
I mean the movie versions

Toys

Give thanks to the wonderful toys
That you buy for your kids
The ones that have their brakes put on
So they can watch them skid

Then there's the one's they throw around
And whallop on the floor
Then one day they throw them too hard
And they go through the door

Finally there are their favourites
Which stay with them all day
They're the ones that suffer the most
As all they eat is clay

Car Trouble

Why do people replace their cars
Just to top each other
One example is the hatchback
Bought by my own brother

When it was new he showed his mates
Which took about three days
Then he went to give it a run
On several motorways

Now one week's over and he's bored
He hasn't gone that far
But to outdo him our neighbour
Has bought a brand new car

Ted

I'd hate to be a teddy bear
That's given to a child
They're often badly beaten up
That's if the owner's mild

They can be grilled or barbecued
If the child thinks they're cold
Or they're sucked 'til they're close to death
And rarely they get old

They're cuddled for ten hours a day
But far too tight to breathe
It's only when they lose themselves
That they will feel relieved

Worst of all for these faithful pals
Is when they're pulled apart
Or when their friend sits on their face
And rides them like a cart

Still they go on with all their love
Until they face the end
They're given to the new baby
And it's endured again

Empty Shelves

I rarely win any trophies
To fill my winner's shelf
I guess I've no one else to blame
It's all down to myself

I think I need a few hobbies
To win myself some gold
I could take ice-skating lessons
But I don't like the cold

Perhaps a team game's what I need
Like lacrosse or hockey
If I had money for a horse
I'd become a jockey

Tennis is a cheap way to start
But we don't have a court
I guess I should just give up now
And keep watching the sport

Waking Nightmare

I woke this morning at half five
With far too little sleep
I tried that useless herbal stuff
But only as it's cheap

I tossed and turned throughout the night
Lay upside down as well
I tried it with the duvet off
And Lavender to smell

I went to sleep in other rooms
On sofas and the sink
Became a monster of the night
Too tired to even think

I thought I'd cracked the sleeping game
At six o'clock a.m.
I settled in the dogs' basket
And nearly growled at them

But half an hour is all I got
Now I can't even try
I've got to leave for work at eight
I'll sleep when I arrive

Broom Cupboard Fantasies

Mr Mop and Mrs Bucket
Were having an affair
They often met up in the park
As it was dark down there

They went there almost twice a week
To get their fix of fun
And usually they got back late
By staying out 'til one

They kept meeting at their spot
They thought that no one knew
Although the partners that they left
Would see each other too

Town Planning

We're lucky to have a theme park
On the edge of our town
It's handy for when the family
Decide they're coming down

It's got a lot of rides inside
Like the roller coaster
It also has a few gift shops
Which sell mugs and posters

There's a section for the children
With some more gentle rides
The teacups are most popular
As well as their big slides

It's open during the summer
Whether it's wet or clear
But I've been there so many times
I doubt I'll go this year

Photographer

I offered to take the photos
At my cousin's party
But by the time the evening came
Everyone was hearty

Uncle Dave did too much dancing
Then threw up on the stage
I had to get a shot of that
Which filled him up with rage

Uncle Bob was touching mum's bum
While they both were dancing
I took a pic of that, and one
With Dad's hand on Francine's

While taking all these photographs
I forgot to do one
There are no photos of myself
But I had loads of fun

New Home

Moving house is a stressful time
As you've lots to prepare
Like packing boxes with your stuff
And fixing broken stairs

You must remember where things go
So they don't end up lost
There's redirecting your post, too
Which all adds to the cost

Bills must be paid before you're gone
Such as the Council Tax
Otherwise they'll catch you up, and
You'll end up wearing sacks

Changing your address is vital
With everyone you know
Subscriptions, banks, clubs and your job
Need to know when you go

When you're at the place of your dreams
You'll feel your heart go boom
It's when you buy your furniture
That there's too little room

Decisions

I hate to have to make a choice
When mealtimes come around
I wish the cook would choose for me
Or make me what they found

There's so much food to consider
So which should I make mine?
Most take longer to cook than eat
This seems a waste of time

I get less hungry when I look
At tins of Veg and stew
Wait – I know what I'll eat this time
I'll have the same as you

Taboo

Many talk about the forbidden
But what does it actually mean?
For some it's having lots of partners
For instance, entire football teams

Some think it's dressing up together
Or using toys once in a while
Others think that wearing PVC
Or leather will make your mate smile

Books and magazines are on the list
Of things that make your parents blush
Drugs are also there, like an Aspirin
To give them a much higher rush

Then there's the crazy, like getting wired
To the speaker on the TV
Stopping your breathing for a short time
Gives apparent intensity

If none of these things appeal to you
And I'll tell you they don't to me
Put three sugars and cream in a cup
And have a forbidden coffee

Check-up

Every January and July
Our dentist checks my teeth
It's only when he's done that I
Can feel any relief

When he has to do a filling
He makes my whole mouth numb
I don't mind when he has to drill
As I can't feel my gums

I chew the inside of my cheeks
Once the filling's been done
I really don't recommend it
As I'm not numb for long

British Institution

There's nothing like a cup of tea
When things are going wrong
It breaks up the play you're watching
When it's gone on too long

It's what you're given when you cry
At someone else's house
It helps to fade the memory
Of Julie with your spouse

And when your team are going down
In an important game
A cup of tea will get you through
The heartbreak and the shame

When life is at its lowest point
And you're not feeling free
You can turn to your faithful chum
A warming cup of tea

Shameless Plug

Helston's a magnificent town
You really have to come
There's just so much to see and do
You can't help but have fun

For children there are loads of parks
Spaced out around the town
Tourist trips for the family
Are vital if you're down

The best time of the year to come
Must be the eighth of May
This is when the people of town
Take part in Flora day

It really is a big event
With dancing through the street
The music played out by the band
Will make you tap your feet

The funfair's set up on this day
With rides and candy floss
There's stalls that sell all sorts of things
And games, like the ring toss

But if this seems too much for you
Then come throughout the year
You'll find the green and peaceful walks
Are bound to keep you here